BEHAVIOR
SOLUTIONS
for the
Inclusive
Classroom

BEHAVIOR SOLUTIONS
for the
Inclusive Classroom

BETH AUNE, OTR/L
BETH BURT & PETER GENNARO

Behavior Solutions for the Inclusive Classroom

All marketing and publishing rights guaranteed to
and reserved by:

FUTURE HORIZONS INC.

721 W. Abram Street
Arlington, Texas 76013
800-489-0727
817-277-0727
817-277-2270 (fax)
E-mail: info@FHautism.com
www.FHautism.com

ISBN: 9781935274087

Printed in the United States of America

Publisher's Cataloging-In-Publication Data
(Prepared by The Donohue Group, Inc.)

Aune, Beth.
    Behavior solutions for the inclusive classroom / Beth Aune, Beth Burt & Peter Gennaro.

    p. : ill. ; cm.

    Includes index.
    ISBN: 978-1-935274-08-7

1. Inclusive education. 2. Mainstreaming in education. 3. Children with disabilities--Education. 4. Classroom management. I. Burt, Beth. II. Gennaro, Peter (Peter L.), 1965- III. Title.

LC1200 .A96 2010

371.9/046

To all parents and educators with an understanding
that one size certainly does not fit all, and that
a child's behavior is the result of our willingness
to be caring, creative, and flexible

Acknowledgements

I dedicate this book, with an endless amount of love and respect, to my three children: Bailey, Riley, and Emma who are the greatest blessings in my life.

I further acknowledge my parents Gene and Lola, my sisters Sharron and Kirsten, my brother Leonard, my colleagues, and my friends who continuously challenge me to achieve my dreams. I am supremely thankful for the numerous uniquely qualified professionals and parents, especially to LOML, who share their knowledge and experience.

And a huge thanks to the true experts—the multitude of special children who remind me daily me how to play, laugh, and cherish each moment for what it is—a joyful gift.

—Beth Aune

Thank you to my sons, Jarren and Koby, and all the other children who fight each day for the "simple things" in life that inspire me to never give up.

A book like this can not exist without the wonderful parents, students, educators, administrators, and other professionals who work so hard each and every day to make school a success for our kids. I am grateful to the parents and teachers who were willing to try these strategies in their classrooms and provide feedback.

My endless love to my husband who made many meals for the family while I obsessed over the manuscript and for his never-ending support. Thank you to my family who always has been there for us—always encouraging, always supporting, and always loving. All my love and thanks to my wonderful girlfriends who bring joy to my life, for their prayers and their reminders to trust in the Lord with all my heart (Pr 3:5).

—**Beth Burt**

I would like to acknowledge those who made it possible for me to have received my own education when I was young; my mother, father, and sister who had the foresight to realize that only with the appropriate education would I find myself in position to choose my future. I want to further acknowledge those teachers and administrators who did more than just present curriculum, but saw within me and others a potential to perhaps affect a positive difference during the short time we are here.

—**Peter Gennaro**

Table of Contents

Introduction

*E*ach year there is a growing emphasis on the inclusion of disabled students into the general education population. As an educator, you will be exposed to students of varying backgrounds, ability levels, and degrees of disability. The National Education Association notes that over the past ten years the number of U.S. students enrolled in special education programs has risen thirty percent, and that three of every four students with disabilities spend part or all of their day in a general education classroom.

Some of your students may come to you with a label: Learning Disability, Autism Spectrum Disorder, Asperger's Syndrome, Sensory Processing Disorder, Tourette Syndrome, or ADD/ADHD. Some of your students may not qualify for services, yet, despite your best efforts, you find that some of them are not responding or attending to your instruction.

The purpose of this book is to offer tools to teachers who have a student or students in their classroom whose behaviors are impeding their learning. Specifically, we are interested in methods for working through the behavioral and academic difficulties that often manifest themselves in a child with the disabilities mentioned above. It is our hope that the content and format of this manual are clear and helpful. We understand that working with this population can at times be a trying experience, and we encourage you to develop well thought-out plans to help you through difficult times. We also encourage you to expand on these ideas and add to them as you become more skilled in working with difficult behaviors. This manual can be a tool for creating such a plan. The ideas presented here come from more than twenty years of experience in working with students with disabilities. The following chapters contain tools designed to get you through the day when difficult behaviors arise. If needed, a written and comprehensive behavior plan should be developed in cooperation with the site team, including the administrator and school psychologist.

Many of the disabilities described in this book are "spectrum disorders," and students on the spectrum share certain characteristics:

- Time concepts present difficulty (before, after, tomorrow, last week, etc.).

- They often don't "get" jokes or ideas behind humorous situations.

- Creativity and imagination can be limited.

- They can be slow to respond.

- They have a difficult time predicting what may happen next, or answering comprehension-type questions.

- Comments may be off track.

- They may have poor handwriting.

- They may have difficulty thinking in a sequential manner.

- They often require a great deal of clarification and one-on-one support.

- They have difficulty remembering sequences in directions or instructions.

- They may often appear forgetful or have poor organizational skills.

- Expressive and receptive language skills are weak.

- They often repeat the same errors.

- They may seem hyperactive or inattentive or easily distracted. They may find it difficult to remain on task for extended periods of time.

- Impulsiveness is common.

- They may show intolerance for frustration and problems in handling day-to-day social interactions and situations; they may overreact to situations.

- They may have difficulty organizing their thoughts for writing assignments or other projects.

- They may engage in self-destructive behavior (head banging, hitting themselves, negative self-talk).

- They may have poor self-esteem.

- They may have difficulty controlling emotions or talking.

- They may have difficulty working with others in groups.

(The behaviors associated with these disabilities are generalizations and do not fit all students on the spectrum.)

We have written this manual in four main sections, each dealing with the most commonly observed behaviors that accompany these disorders: 1) movement issues; 2) avoidance and retreat behaviors; 3) difficulty with routine and academics; and 4) social-emotional issues. We are not suggesting that all behavioral issues connected to these disorders can be neatly categorized, nor are we attempting to "cure" the disability. We are primarily interested in helping teachers get through particular problems they may encounter during the course of their day. In other words, if the child does A, we suggest that the teacher does B in order to alleviate the problem, and then continue with the school tasks at hand for the benefit of all students.

Please keep in mind that the difficulties that these students face can (and often do) change daily—sometimes with no explanation. It is our hope you will individualize the suggestions we have presented, based on each child's needs.

Many districts are employing response to intervention (RtI) for behavior. The authors feel this manual is an appropriate grounding for tier one and tier two interventions.

While we describe many disabling conditions in this book, we hope that the suggestions can transfer to all students demonstrating difficult behaviors—regardless of whether or not they are diagnosed with a disability.

Section One

Movement Issues

*L*earning and paying attention depend upon the ability to integrate and organize information from our senses. We are all familiar with the five basic senses: sight, hearing, taste, smell, and touch. But there are other senses that are not as familiar, including the sense of movement and the sense of muscle-awareness. A student's inability to organize sensory input creates a traffic jam in his or her brain, making it difficult to pay attention and learn. To be successful learners, our senses must work together in an organized manner.

Children with disabilities often have difficulty interpreting information from their environment and even from their own bodies. Children who are under-aware will often use strategies such as excessive movement and touching to gather additional information. They may seek out constant stimulation or more intense and prolonged sensory input by taking part in disruptive activities or moving constantly.

Some behaviors seen in these children include:

- Hyperactivity or fidgeting, as they seek more sensation

- Insensitivity to touch or pain, or touching others too often or too hard (which may appear to be aggressive behavior)

- Taking part in unsafe activities, such as climbing too high or using equipment incorrectly

- Craving sounds that are too loud, such as when listening to radio or TV

Behavior?

Arm- & Hand-Flapping

Arm- or hand-flapping tends to occur when a student feels anxious or lacks the ability to express concerns or emotions appropriately. However, these motions may also occur when a student is genuinely happy or excited about something. This stereotypical behavior looks odd, and thus can socially isolate a student from his peers.

Arm- or hand-flapping is often used as a calming method, and is different from swinging one's arms. (See the next topic for more information regarding arm-swinging.)

Solutions!

- This is among the most difficult behaviors to replace. It is best to **teach other students to expect such behavior occasionally.** With this understanding, they will be less likely to pay attention to it.

- **Teach the student to replace the flapping** with a similar, but less conspicuous, behavior. For example, the student could play with a fidget toy to keep his hands occupied (large pockets on a loose jacket or hooded sweatshirt are great for concealing a fidget toy). Or, the student can use isometric exercises such as pressing palms together or lightly bumping one of his fists against his palm.

- The student can use a familiar object—such as a pencil—to **keep his hands busy.** (See Appendix B for a list of sensory input devices.)

- Try to anticipate times of stress or excitement, and **allow the student to perform a "movement activity"** (see Appendix A).

Behavior?

Arm-Swinging

Kids who swing their arms use this either as a regulatory movement to aid calming, or they simply enjoy and seek out movement. They have difficulty keeping still when required to do so, like when standing in line or waiting for a turn.

Solutions!

- If the arm-swinging is bothering people, **redirect**. Explain to the student why it is not appropriate (it looks odd, or it might hurt someone, etc.). Then ask the student to stop or to put his hands in his pockets.

- If the student is in line waiting for an activity, **place him at the end** of the line where he will be less of a disruption.

- **Give the student a task** that requires that they hold onto something to keep their hands and arms busy.

Behavior?

Breaking Pencils and/or Crayons

$\int$ ome students experience poor or incomplete feedback from their muscles or joints. These students' pencils or crayons often break because they don't realize how heavily they are pressing down. Or they may turn in their papers full of holes due to heavy erasing. Other students may become frustrated because one student keeps breaking the crayons. If you notice a student who uses the pencil sharpener excessively, keep in mind that he or she may be one of those children receiving poor or incomplete feedback from muscles or joints.

Solutions!

- **Use heavy-duty writing/drawing implements.** Pencils and crayons that are less likely to break under heavy pressure are available. If the student is old enough, you can encourage him to use a pen. While this makes correcting errors more difficult, it gives him an option that can be less frustrating.

- Consider having the student **switch to a "mechanical pencil."** It can help raise awareness of the amount of force being placed on the writing utensil.

- If possible, **use a heavier paper** that won't tear as easily when the student erases. Also, let him "line out" errors (without penalty) rather than erase them.

- If the student is old enough, **experiment with keyboard instruments.** These typing devices can be used in the classroom, they are affordable, and they offer the student the opportunity to turn in neatly corrected work.

● If the student is receiving occupational therapy (OT) services, **let the therapist know** about the problem; he or she may offer helpful suggestions or work with you on a solution. (Check with the Case Manager first. Your district will have guidelines for special education occupational therapy referrals.)

Bumping Into Other Students/Touching

You may observe this behavior in many different settings from preschool through high school. During circle time, a student may want to lie down or kick his neighbor. This student is in other people's space. Such students have a hard time keeping their hands to themselves, often touching other students' bodies or hair.

These students may also have a hard time lining up, or staying in line. You may notice them with their hand out, running their fingers against the walls as the line moves down the hallway. These may also be the students who are

always bumping into others in line or during circle time, sometimes hurting others. They will often apologize after the teacher points it out, but they continue to be unaware of their actions. This is because they are under-sensitive to touch, or unaware of their body's position in space.

Solutions!

- **Remind the student of the rules of personal space.** If you know you have a student with these issues, it is best to include lessons at the beginning of the year that emphasize the importance of maintaining a proper distance from his peers during the day. The student may have already received this training in counseling or at home. When you know that the student is aware of the rules of personal space, a prompt is often enough to eliminate the behavior, at least for a period of time.

- If the student is unable to stop the behavior, even with prompts, it may be necessary to allow him an opportunity to get his need met in a more appropriate manner. **Movement breaks can be used** in these situations. A pass to get a drink or use the restroom can work well here. (See Appendix A.)

For some students, it is necessary that they have some prior knowledge of personal space rules. Then a prompt from the teacher or playground supervisor can often be enough to eliminate the behavior for a period of time. Several prompts may be needed during the course of the day. If the prompts are ineffective, try the movement breaks as described in Appendix A. The more these students have the opportunity to use these techniques, the more they will seek them out before initiating inappropriate or disruptive behavior.

Behavior?

Chewing on Shirt or Other Inappropriate Items

*O*ne coping mechanism for self-regulation used by students is to chew on their shirt, causing holes or large wet spots. Some of these students also often chew their erasers or continually bite on pencils. Oral input is organizing and calming (as when an infant sucks on a pacifier, or an adult chews gum). It is important to provide them access to that input in a way that is socially acceptable and age-appropriate.

Solutions!

- **Allow the student to eat food in the classroom while working. Chewy foods** such as Jolly Ranchers®, Starburst® candies, fruit rolls, or gummy bears can give a student the oral stimulation and sensory input that is needed to keep him alert and on task. **Crunchy foods** such as pretzels, vegetables, or granola bars can also be effective, although the noise created can be a distraction for the surrounding students. **Sour foods** such as lemon balls can also achieve the desired effect.

- **Allow the student to drink from a water bottle that has a large plastic straw.** It is common to see students with water bottles at their desks, so the student will blend in well with his classmates. He can achieve the needed oral input by chewing or sucking the straw without appearing odd, or "different."

● **For younger students (Kindergarten and below), It is possible to use a length of aquarium hose or Chewy-Tubes for the student to chew on.** Students this age are less socially aware, and there is less of a stigma on the child who uses such a device.

The key here is to replace the socially unacceptable behavior of chewing on shirts (or pencils) with chewing on objects that are less likely to stigmatize the student. As educators, we must not let established policy be a substitute for wise and successful decision-making. Should a "No Food" policy exist in your classroom, you may need to be willing to make adjustments for the benefit of the student with a disability, and the rest of the class, as well. Remember, educators have greater decision-making control than the students whose disability causes inappropriate behaviors. As educators, we have the ability to adjust our responses to the student whose disability results in disruptive or inappropriate behavior.

Behavior?

Excessive Yawning

How frustrating is it to be giving a lesson, only to look up and see a student yawning continuously? Is the child not getting enough sleep? Is the lesson really boring? Yawning can be a sign that the body is under-aroused. In this case, it is best to provide the student opportunities to get the input needed to keep her body and mind alert.

Solutions!

- **Allow the student to drink water from a water bottle** (many teachers already allow this in their classes). This gives the student the opportunity to move her body in an appropriate manner and get the input needed to remain alert and focused.

- **Allow movement breaks.** Some teachers have worked out a system that gives the student the chance to occasionally get up from her seat and get a drink, or to put some papers on the teacher's desk. These opportunities for physical movement can often help the student avoid excessive stretching and yawning. (See Appendix A for more suggestions.)

- **Alternate movement breaks with allowing the student to eat sour candy** such as lemon balls, **or crunchy foods** such as dry cereal or pretzels. This input is arousing and organizing. (For a complete list of foods, see Appendix B.)

Again, much of what is being suggested assumes that the student in question has the level of maturity to handle the additional responsibility. With this in mind, make decisions wisely.

Behavior?

Fidgeting

The child who fidgets at his desk has some of the same movement issues we have discussed on previous pages. The craving for movement can lead a student to tap pencils or fingers, lean over his desk, shake the desk, or tense his body. An even stronger craving for movement can lead to rocking, jumping up and down, and swinging his arms. These movements can actually help the student to remain on task and pay attention when directed.

Solutions!

- **Place the student at the end of an aisle or row of chairs.** Accept the fact that you cannot eliminate the behavior one-hundred percent, and move him to a position in class where he will be the least distracting to his peers, without isolating him from them.

- **Allow the student to occasionally stand at his desk** while working. This is harmless, and the student can be quietly directed to sit back down after an agreed-upon amount of time has elapsed.

- **Provide the student with a fidget toy,** such as a squeeze ball. This can give the student the sensory input needed to keep him focused.

- **Give the student a Movement Break** with a goal-directed activity. (See Appendix B for a list of suggested activities.)

- **Allow the student to have crunchy or sour food** as a replacement for fidgeting.

- **Allow access to a seat cushion device** (if age-appropriate) such as a Movin' Sit or Disc'O'Sit. These semi-inflatable devices allow movement while keeping the chair stable. Allow enough movement for the student to gain the input needed to stay focused without resorting to fidgeting that could bother classmates and disrupt classroom progress.

Remember—some fidgeting is okay. We all do it!

Behavior?

Out-of-Seat Behaviors

Some students have a stronger need to move around than others. They will devise excuses to get up from their seats and move about. They may "need" to sharpen their pencils several times an hour, or go to the restroom or get a drink of water. Or they may wander around the room, pretending to look for a book or at what other students are doing. Other behaviors may not be as socially appropriate, such as jumping up and down, pacing, or stomping. However, these "kinesthetic" students may simply be trying to get some of their sensory needs met.

Solutions!

- **Ask the student to run an errand for you outside of class** The teacher can have pre-written hall passes stashed in her drawer so that when she sees the kinesthetic student begin to fidget, she can call on him to carry a message for her to another teacher (preferably one whose classroom or office is on the opposite side of the building!) She can quietly let him know that it is also okay for him to stop at the water fountain or the restroom.

- The sealed envelope does not have to contain legitimate business—the two teachers will have talked previously, so the second teacher expects to periodically see this student "deliver" something. She simply accepts the envelope and continues whatever she was doing.

- Another idea would be to **have the student do a manual task in the classroom.** Such tasks could include moving books from one side of the class-room to the other, storing/taking out backpacks or play equipment, wiping/erasing the whiteboard, stapling/hole-punching papers, and sorting home-work or other papers into files or boxes. In addition to helping complete classroom chores, it makes the student feel needed while he is simultaneously get-ting the sensory input he requires.

- Depending on the age of the child, it might be ap-propriate to **use a weighted vest or lap weight** to help him get the deep pressure needed to get him through a difficult time. Weighted equipment can help the student feel "grounded," and he can have ac-cess to these things while sitting at his desk.

- If a playground supervisor or special education as-sistant is available to supervise the child, **allow him to go outside and "work out" on the playground equipment** for about five minutes. If the student is working with an OT, check with him or her to learn the most effective activities.

The solution to most problems with a kinesthetic stu-dent is to help him focus his mind by allowing his body's sensory needs be met for a short period of time. Once this has been accomplished, the student will be able to re-engage in class activities.

Behavior?

Excessive Hugging, Leaning against People, or Pushing People

The student with sensory needs may find that he can get these needs met by leaning against or pushing people or objects. In an attempt to fulfill these needs, he may try to hug others at inappropriate times, or engage in desk-pushing or foot stomping while walking. This is also called deep-pressure seeking. The student uses these techniques to "ground" or calm himself.

$$\longrightarrow$$

Solutions!

● As with many other sensory issues, **providing movement breaks** for the student can be of great benefit. Passing out papers or books, or running an errand often accomplishes the goal of getting sensory needs met—and does so in an appropriate manner.

● When it is age-appropriate, **use a weighted vest or lap weight** to give the student access to the deep pressure he craves. Your special education Case Manager or occupational therapist can provide these devices.

● **Encourage the use of isometric exercises** such as hand-clasps or wall-pushing.

● **Remind the student of the rules of personal space.** Some teachers use the concept of an invisible bubble around everyone (some people's bubbles are larger than others).

- **Use oral strategies:** Give the student something that is difficult to chew, such as taffy, or hard caramel.

Behavior?

Taking Off Shoes

When children have sensory deficits that affect their sense of touch, it is often difficult to find shoes that feel comfortable to them. Sometimes the shoes feel so uncomfortable to these children that they become distracted—to an extent that they are not able to concentrate on anything else. This discomfort may cause them to take off their shoes at inappropriate times. Children with this sensory profile often prefer to go barefoot or wear sandals, both of which may violate school safety standards.

Solutions!

- **Allow the student to temporarily keep her shoes off** (while keeping her socks on) in the classroom. While some teachers may deem this inappropriate, it is generally harmless to allow this behavior for a short period of time.

- Encourage the student to tie her shoes loosely.

- **Set firm boundaries**. There will be some circumstances or areas in which the child must not take off her shoes. It helps to explain clearly to the child why the rule must be enforced in these cases: 1) when taking off shoes might offend others (e.g., in the cafeteria where food is served), or 2) on the playground where they could be injured by stepping on a sharp object.

Understand the need behind the behavior. If we as educators ignore the need, it may lead to behaviors that are far more distracting than the taking off of shoes. Above all, be open to such ideas as are mentioned in this section. It can help you, the student, and the rest of the class.

Section Two

Avoidance and Retreat Behaviors

In the previous section we discussed some of the issues observed with students who are *under*-responsive to sensation. This section will address the issues seen with children who are *over*-responsive to sensation.

Tactile defensiveness, or hyper-responsiveness to touch, was identified by OT Dr. Jean Ayers in the 1960s. These children's nervous systems feel sensation too intensely and they feel as though they are constantly being bombarded with information. Consequently, they often have a "fight, fright, or flight" response to sensations—a condition called

"sensory defensiveness." They may try to avoid or minimize sensations by avoiding being touched or by being very particular about clothing and foods.

The simple acts of getting them ready for school—combing, brushing, shampooing hair, cutting fingernails, or brushing teeth—can be exhausting for the families of these children, who may react defensively by acting out or throwing a tantrum. Other children may insist on wearing only clothing of a certain texture, with all the tags removed, or will eat only a limited number of foods because of intolerance to textures. Social interactions can be severely limited because the child withdraws or becomes aggressive when touched unexpectedly.

These children may:

- Respond to being touched with aggression or withdrawal

- Fear movement and heights, or get sick from exposure to movement and heights

- Be very cautious and unwilling to take risks or try new things

Feel uncomfortable in loud or busy environments such as playgrounds, cafeterias, classrooms, or school assemblies

 Be very picky eaters and/or overly sensitive to food smells

We all have a unique sensory profile. Some of us are distracted or overwhelmed by loud noises, visual chaos, or someone standing too close. Sometimes we get drowsy when sitting too long in place, as during a lecture. We may unconsciously tap our pencil, bounce our foot, or put a piece of gum in our mouth.

The difference between us and kids with disabilities or immature central nervous systems is that the kids experience these distractions at a much higher level than we do, and they often use strategies that are inappropriate at school.

Avoiding Physical Contact or Messy Activities

*A*nn is a Kindergartner who seemed to be doing well in class. One day during art class, the teacher announced that the class would be finger-painting. Ann slowly walked over to the table and looked at the paint. When the teacher asked her to put her hands into the paint, she refused. Then the teacher tried taking Ann's hand and submerging it in the paint. Ann suddenly became aggressive—hitting, kicking, and scratching.

Tactile defensiveness, or hyper-responsiveness to touch, was identified by OT Jean Ayers in the 1960s. A child with sensory defensiveness typically has a highly aroused nervous system that does not recognize when input is non-threatening, but nevertheless prepares the body for survival. Behaviors associated with tactile defensiveness are aggressiveness, avoidance, withdrawal, and intolerance of daily routines.

A student's behavioral and emotional responses to certain types of tactile stimuli can seem negative and out of proportion. After all, those same stimuli do not seem to bother others. Nevertheless, children with tactile defensiveness may not be able to tolerate hugging, certain touches (hard or light), or putting their hands into paint or glue.

Solutions!

● **Encourage, but do not force the child to participate.**

● **Explore alternatives.** Let the child use glue sticks instead of glue, or a paintbrush instead of finger painting. Avoid forcing the child; it could cause her to go into "overload" and have a violent or fearful reaction.

● If a child has a hard time with physical contact, **consider placing her at the beginning or end of a row of desks,** where it is less likely she will have physical contact with others. In the case of a very young child, place her near peers who have a calm nature.

● **Reinforce the child for making genuine attempts** to participate, and seek to increase tolerance over time.

Behavior?

Covering Ears

John was sitting in the classroom working at his desk when the fire alarm went off. John screamed, covered his ears, and ran out of the room. Negative responses (such as fear, withdrawal, etc.) to sounds and noises can be the result of auditory defensiveness. Some children fear the sound of vacuum cleaners, lawn mowers, hair dryers, leaf blowers, sirens, and toilets flushing. Parents sometimes have to arrange to use these appliances when the child is out of earshot.

→

So how do these students cope with the many sounds at school, such as fire drills, school bells, morning announcement, and music? Some students may show intolerance by clapping their hands over their ears, becoming upset or crying. However, steps can be taken to make such situations less stressful for these students.

Solutions!

- If possible, **give the student warning** that certain sounds are going to occur. Most teachers know in advance when fire drills will take place, for example. If the student has fair warning, the fear or confusion that might otherwise accompany such noises may be lessened, or avoided completely.

- If appropriate (for younger students), the use of ear-plugs or headphones may help the student work independently and avoid outside distractions.

● If the student has difficulty in noisy lunchrooms or assembly hall, **consider allowing him to have an alternate plan.** For instance, taking lunch in the RSP room or office can take some of the pressure off the student. Often, just knowing that an option *exists* can ease tension.

● **Work with the student to formulate a "plan"** for when certain noises occur. For instance, when the fire drill starts, if the student knows exactly what to do, he will have a goal-oriented task to complete. Thus occupied, his mind will be diverted from the stressful situation instead of going automatically into "flight" mode.

● If the day-to-day bustle of the classroom is becoming difficult for the student, **allow him to take a "Noise Break."** This can be accomplished several ways: He could use headphones at the computer, or ear-plugs while reading, for example. It's important to allow the student to have a "quiet place" during these times.

Hiding or Running Away When Upset

A student looks into his lunch box, sees that something is missing, lets out a loud cry and bolts for the door. Students who hide or run away when upset are displaying the "flight" response. These students may react to a seemingly ordinary event as if their lives were on the line. Confusion, lack of ability to problem-solve, and emotional buildup can trigger this response. It is when the student is presented with the unexpected, or something out of the ordinary, that he is most likely to display this behavior.

When these events occur, the student can appear markedly different from his peers. He is smart enough to know the rules, but is willfully not following them due to unexpected events that may appear trivial and unimportant to us, but seem monumental to him. Do not take this behavior personally. It frequently is a reaction to too much stimulation. Your first response should be to get the student somewhere he feels safe, so he can "regroup." Only after he has been given enough time to settle down will he be able to communicate his distress to you. Attempting to force communication when he is over-stimulated will lead to an even more intense escalation.

Solutions!

- **Being alone can be restorative.** Do not force the child into a crowded situation until he is ready to return. Allow him time away from the situation (in the office, Resource Room, or another designated "safe place") until he has de-escalated.

● **Try to help the student "burn up" some of the emotional energy** that has been put in motion by the triggering event. A vigorous walk or time on the swing can help.

● **Use pre-selected rules or stories** to assist the student back into his routine. Encourage him to use a preset plan the next time he has those feelings.

● **Attempt to identify and predict when such times will occur.** If your experience tells you, for instance, that the confusion of a fire drill brings out these responses in the student, take steps to see that he is prepared ahead of time.

● **Above all, do not take the behavior personally.** Under stress, kids can often say inappropriate things that they do not mean.

Putting Head Down, or "Shutting Down"

A student may isolate herself by putting her head down or by simply "shutting down." She may physically isolate herself by reading a book at an inappropriate time, or by body language—turning her back on others, for example. Like the student who chooses "flight" as a response to stress, she may choose to isolate herself from peers due to a lack of social abilities. If she doesn't have the ability to initiate friendship or conversation, "choosing" to be off by herself often offers a comfortable alternative. These students are often working very hard, not only academically, but also trying to maintain their sensory systems, trying to

$$\longrightarrow$$

remember all the social "rules," and learning how to work with others.

- If the student is putting her head down or seems to be "shutting down" in class, **give her a few moments to collect herself.** Then you may want to approach her and redirect.

- Remember that **being alone can be restorative.** Allow her time away from the situation (the office or Resource Room can serve as a location where there is supervision and she can get away from the problem area) until she is ready to re-engage.

- If she is isolating herself because she does not know what to say or do in a social situation, **she may have to learn a story or a set of social rules that can help her interact with others.** Consult with the site's speech/language therapist or special education case manager for information on social stories.

Section Three

Difficulty with Routine and Academics

A variety of causes can decrease a student's ability to function competently in the classroom. A child who is tired, sick, or hungry can have problems adhering to the class routine or academics. However, with a student on the autism spectrum (or other disabling conditions), other issues can also have an effect.

- **Internal Issues:** not being understood; not understanding; not having enough information; not having adequate skills for a task; not having choices; fear of making a mistake; being corrected; being denied,

interrupted, late, or ignored; fear of being teased, scolded, or left out.

- **External Issues:** changes in the environment or routine: small schedule changes; location changes, staff or teacher being absent or late; a friend or family member not coming; anticipating an event or activity; cancellation of an event or activity; or having to wait too long.

- **Environmental Confusion:** crowds, noise, too much movement; too much visual stimuli; not having enough space; or losing things of value.

- **Organizational Issues:** Regardless of their intelligence, many students with disabilities have trouble with organizational skills. Even a straight-A student may be incapable of remembering to bring a pencil to class, or forget the deadline for an assignment.

- **Sensory Issues:** A student may have trouble regulating his or her body, or sitting still and focusing on an assignment.

Do not take misbehavior personally. Children with Autism Spectrum Disorders, Learning Disabilities or Tourette Syndrome are not manipulative, scheming children who are trying to make life difficult. They are seldom, if ever, capable of being manipulative. Usually, their misbehavior is the result of efforts to survive experiences that may be confusing, disorienting, or frightening. Most of these students have extreme difficulty reading the reactions of others, and have poor problem-solving skills.

Behavior?

Difficulty with Carpet Time

*C*arpet-time issues can be a result of sensory deficits. The child may not be sure where his body is, or he may need more movement to keep him alert. He may be uncomfortable with sitting in a large group of children. The group could be too loud, or have too many smells, which results in sensory overload. There are several strategies that can be effective in these situations. You may have to try them to see which is effective for your student,

Solutions!

- **Use a visual cue to show the student where the boundaries are.** Rather than making a request to "Keep your hands to yourself," try coupling the request with a visual. For example, you can use a small square of carpet to indicate where the student sits, and let him know that he is to remain entirely within that square during carpet time. Use verbal prompts and reminders to supplement the visual cue. Alternately, you could tape off a square of the same size. The key is to give visual boundaries to the student while also giving verbal prompts as reminders.

- **Allow the student to have something in his or her hands, such as a squeeze-ball.** This is often enough to give the student the sensory input needed to make it through the lesson.

- **Strategically place the child in a location where he or she is less likely to be disturbed.** This will most likely be a front or back corner of the group. There the student will not have the distraction of having other students on all sides of him. It is also recommended that less "active" children be placed in proximity to this student in these situations—also to limit distractions. Since each child is different, you may want to try different areas of the group until the optimal location is found.

● **Consider allowing the student to sit on a small chair** to help him keep his body to himself.

The goal is to have the carpet-activity dynamics planned out before they begin. If the student can start out with the visual cues of limitation (the carpet square), and be placed in an area where distraction is less likely, the likelihood of problems may decrease.

Behavior?

Difficulty with Lining Up

*P*eter is a third grade student who does well in class. However, when the bell rings and recess is over, instead of lining up with the rest of his class, he goes running out into the field. Why?

Most typical students learn that, on the playground, when the bell rings, it is a signal for the class to "line up." Sometimes there can be fifty to a hundred students rushing to find their place in the appropriate line. For some students, this scenario can be a nightmare. They are immediately overwhelmed by the noise of the bell and the large

53

number of students rushing around. Some simple planning can help alleviate these difficulties and, while they may not eliminate them altogether, they can lessen their severity.

- **A brief reminder to the student that a "line up" is set to begin** can eliminate any surprise or perceived structural breakdown. If the student knows that within, say, two minutes, he will need to take his place in line, the shock of disorganization that accompanies such times can be reduced. On the playground, this task can be assigned to a yard-duty supervisor.

- **Assign the student a permanent place in line.** This gives him a plan to follow, and a structured goal. Some teachers have reported that assigning the student to the first or last place in line usually works best. This way, the student has one other child in front of or behind him, instead of being "surrounded" by having students in front *and* behind. Other teachers have reported success by assigning the student the third place in line. This way, other students won't resent never having a chance to be first, and will hold the child's place in line more readily.

- **Allow the student to get in line after the others have lined up.** The student needs to understand that hiding or wandering away is unacceptable, but you can allow him the opportunity to get in line after most of the chaos has subsided.

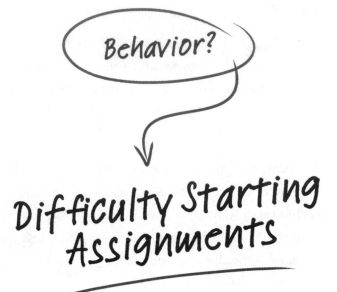

Difficulty Starting Assignments

Instead of doing class work that was assigned to him, the student may be reading a book. This may happen five times a day or more. Why? Students with learning disabilities or Autism Spectrum Disorders usually have difficulties with problem-solving, abstract and conceptual thinking, and organization. These students are capable of doing the work, but may need a little more guidance from the teacher.

Solutions!

● You may need to **offer additional explanation.** Remember, these students have a hard time with abstract ideas and relationships. You may need to simplify the question.

● **Reduce the number of choices** so the student has fewer options to weigh. For instance, if the assignment is to write about "What I Did Last Summer," consider changing it (for this student) to something more specific, such as "Explain what it was like getting swimming lessons last summer." Of course, this assumes that you have some background information about the student, and such background information is a must. Working closely with the family and case manager can help in this area.

● **Use visual clues.** Depending on the assignment, ask the class to brainstorm ideas and write their responses on the board or have the student use a graphic organizer. This gives the student a visual array of ideas to choose from, and can help the entire class.

- Because many students with disabilities have difficulty in the area of planning, try pre-planning the assignment. **Ask the student specific questions** such as "What materials will you need to have?" (pencil, paper, etc.), and "What should you do first?"

- Proximity can be a useful tool in these cases. Some students need only a slight nudge from the "velvet hammer" to begin the task. **Make it a point to walk near the student after directing the class to begin a task so you can ask and answer clarifying questions.**

- Create a brainstorming session with the entire class to narrow down the choices.

Behavior?

Difficulty with Small Group Activities

Students with disabilities may have a difficult time participating in small-group activities. You may have a student who doesn't want to come to circle time, or prefers to sit away from others. Even in smaller groups, or when paired up with another student, this child may not talk, or may want to sit with someone else. Again, because of these students' organizational, problem-solving, and/or sensory issues, planning ahead can help during times of cooperative learning.

Solutions!

- **Avoid allowing the students to pick their own group members.** Not only does this tend to be chaotic, it also means that the student with disabilities must approach classmates and initiate a conversation, which can cause great anxiety. Additionally, these students are often the last to be "picked" by peer groups, which contributes to feelings of isolation.

- Give some thought to which group would best ease the difficulties of the student. **Choose group partners who are leaders and can give structured direction without pushing or ignoring the student with the disability.** Encourage these partners to get input from all members of the group before moving on to other tasks.

- **Set group goals and guidelines prior to allowing the class to form into groups.** For example:

assign individual roles and responsibilities, such as recorder, reporter, etc. This gives all students goal-oriented tasks to complete before the "chaos" of the class rearranging itself into small groups.

Behavior?

Difficulty with Homework

Many parents report that the issue of homework becomes a battleground. They say homework that should have taken thirty minutes to complete took three times that long—with the parents having to sit next to the child the entire time. There are a number of theories about why this happens. Some of the problem could be a lack of organizational skills. The student becomes anxious at the thought of having to do the work and, subsequently, can't organize and focus his mind. Or it may be related to the student's rigidity: school is for work; home is for fun. Or perhaps the student has other ideas about how to spend his time, and doesn't understand why schoolwork has to interfere. Still other students may feel that, since they understand the concept, there is no need to practice.

- Ask the parents if they **have a structured routine for homework.** As much as possible, homework should be done in the same place, and at the same time, every day.

- **Prioritize homework.** If the parents need to limit the amount of homework that is being done, what is the most important? Is it more important that the student writes spelling words five times each, or that he writes the spelling words two times each, and completes the math? For math homework, if the format allows, allow the student to complete all the odd or even problems instead of the entire page, or enough of the problems to show mastery.

● Work with the parents to **set an appropriate time limit for homework.** If the student is supposed to be doing thirty minutes a night, ask the parents to set a timer for thirty minutes. As long as the student works successfully, and an appropriate amount has been completed, at the end of thirty minutes the homework will be considered done.

Losing Materials and Missing Assignments

*B*ecause these students generally have planning deficits, what to do with a completed assignment or previously used materials is something the student may not take into consideration. Once the task is done or the items have been used, they are stuffed into a desk or a backpack, and the student goes on to the next subject. By the time the items are needed again, they are nowhere to be found. These students are the ones who are always looking for a pencil or an assignment instead of listening to the instructions you are giving, and they always seem to be playing "catch up." They may be missing homework or class assignments—not because the work hasn't been completed, but because they cannot locate the proper papers.

- **Teach the class a general system for organizing work and storing materials.** Don't assume that every student knows where to put his or her papers.

- Make it a point to **verbally prompt the student after each lesson to put his assignment and other materials in their proper location.** More importantly, do not allow the student to go on to the next subject until you have seen the items put where they need to go. This sounds like a cumbersome task, but once it becomes habit, you may find yourself using it with several of your students.

- Make it a point at the beginning of the day to nonchalantly **pull the student aside** and ask him to open his backpack and give you the homework assignment. This is considered *prompting the student*.

- **Have a consistent location for storing materials** such as pencil boxes, etc.

- At the end of each day, **use a peer buddy or teacher's aide to help the student make certain that all needed materials and homework assignments are in order** prior to leaving school.

- **Enlist the parents' help** in practicing the same methods at home so assignments and materials will arrive at school in order.

- **Make certain that all homework assignments are written on the board** and the student has copied them down—and stored them in his or her folder successfully. This way the parents will have less difficulty assisting them with completion.

- Teachers may also want to **copy the overhead transparencies** they used in class for teaching and for the agenda. This helps parents be more informed and able to communicate with their child about school.

- If a child is prone to losing papers, have a plan. Have a list of other students the child can call. **Some teachers put their homework assignments on the internet.**

Behavior?

Having a Messy Desk or Disorganized Binder

Again, we see lack of organizational skills impacting school.

Solutions!

- **Teach the class a general system for organizing work and storing materials.** Have a regularly scheduled time that the entire class can organize their desks and binders. Set clear expectations.

- **Have a consistent place to store materials.** You may consider putting a picture or label where each item belongs.

- **Make it as simple as possible.** If the student is having problems with a folder for every subject, simplify. Use one binder with only two pockets—one for completed work, and another for work that is to be turned in.

- **Set up a review system**—either with a peer or with parents—to ensure the binder is in order every night.

⬤ **Have the student be an active participant** in developing his organizational strategies. We often teach organizational skills in a way that works for us, rather than helping the student identify what works best for him. He will be much more likely to remember and implement his *own* ideas.

Behavior?

Poor Handwriting

Some students have poor fine-motor ability and planning skills. They may also press too hard or too softly when writing. Additionally, they may have difficulty staying within the lines or have spacing issues. All of these perceptual and planning problems affect a student's work.

Some of these students may be more interested in simply completing the assigned task than taking the time to do it in an orderly fashion. This rush to complete a task often leads to writing that is difficult to decipher, and is not indicative of the child's true ability.

Solutions!

- **Allow the student to chew gum during writing assignments.** The sensory input and rhythm created by chewing can be calming, to the point that the student can focus on the outcome.

- **Allow additional time for the student to complete a writing task.** If the student understands that he is not under time constraints, he may be able to relax and achieve the desired outcome.

- **Explore alternatives to traditional writing practices.** Allow oral reports; or give the student access to a Calcuscribe or AlphaSmart.

- **Provide the student with weighted pencils and pens, or thicker crayons**. These specialty products can be of use for students with fine motor issues.

- To help control the size and uniformity of letters, **draw guides on paper with a marker, or use paper** with raised lines that provide clear vertical and horizontal boundaries. Typical notebook paper has faint lines that do not provide enough of a boundary for the child.

- **Allow the child to take a break between lines to aid in attending.**

- Emphasize quality over quantity.

- **Give the child extra practice** with motor patterning, tracing, and copying.

Behavior?

Not Attending/Off Task or Not Following Directions

*T*here are quite a few issues involved in attention. For instance, just because a student isn't looking at you does not mean he is not paying attention to what you are saying.

Some students may have ADD in combination with another disability—they may truly have an issue with staying on task. However, many students without ADD can pay attention, but have difficulty regulating and shifting their attention. This could be the student who seems distracted after coming in from recess and has a hard time settling

down. Or it could be the student who would prefer to finish reading a book rather than start a new lesson. These students are usually engaged in something else—whether it is their own thought process or trying to finish a previous assignment—and are having difficulty transitioning to the next area of focus.

Some of these students may appear to be "daydreaming." These students could be battling sensory overload, weak auditory processing (which makes following verbal directions difficult), or they may simply have motivations that are different from those of typical students. Going off into their own thoughts is much more pleasurable to them than receiving an "A" on a test. Or the student may be "stuck"— he doesn't know what to do or say next, or understand how to ask for help.

Solutions!

● For students who are over-stimulated by the environment, **provide quiet space** where they can "regroup."

● **Use visual cues.** Have a written or picture-schedule of directions.

● Redirect through a signal, touch, a peer buddy, or by asking questions.

● **Help the child plan out a task.** Ask "What materials do you need" and "What do you do first?" Break down assignments into manageable portions.

● Work on limiting compulsive thoughts. **Set limits on how long the child may perseverate.**

● As needed, **allow the child to eat crunchy or chewy foods or drink from a water bottle, or drink through a straw**, to help with focus and organization.

● A child's hands are excellent modulators for arousals states, and can help modulate attending and focusing. (**Try squeeze-balls, Koosh® balls, paper clips, Silly Putty®, or Theraputty™.**)

● **Seat the child at the front of the class** to minimize distractions.

● **Set up a signal** or a sentence the child can say when he needs help.

● Allow the student to work in shorter sessions, with frequent breaks.

● **Find ways to reinforce the child for paying attention.** This can range from material reinforcement (candy, stickers) to social reinforcement (praising, hugging). You might even allow the child to play with a favorite toy, go for a walk, swing, or simply have some time alone.

Behavior?

Not Following Playground Rules

The playground is supposed to be a place of relaxation and fun for students, but for the child with a disability, it can be the worst part of the day. One scenario involves the student with sensory issues. This student has been trying to maintain in the classroom all morning and then he gets a chance to "play." His body is crying out for deep pressure—the kind you get by jumping, swinging and climbing. His body needs a lot of it, and he isn't prepared to share the equipment with a hundred other students. Students like this may break the rules trying to get their sensory needs met. They can become

over-stimulated and refuse to stop playing, or they may run away.

Some children may break the rules for social reasons. Many of these students have poor motor skills, making it difficult to play games like soccer, kickball, basketball, or handball. They may become frustrated—wanting to join in the games, but not being able to play. They may wander off to an area that is considered "off limits," looking for solitude. This behavior can *seem* disrespectful. These students "know" the rules, yet seem to purposely disregard them.

Students with Autism Spectrum Disorders are usually rule-driven. They like structure and routine. Breaking the rules can be an indication that they are overwhelmed and trying to get a particular need met such as a sensory need. Or they are trying to avoid a situation by running away. Geraldine Robertson, an adult with Asperger's Syndrome, described the playground like this. "They told me I would have friends, but the playground was a nightmare of noise and fighting, lying, cheating, and people going fast—everyone knowing what to do but me. It was like a flock of birds wheeling, surging, changing direction at a whim, all knowing what to do, and all in unison except for one at the back. Me. I had to watch and anticipate and follow, so I was never in harmony. Sometimes I got left behind, and there were hawks out there. I didn't know how to tell who was a friend" (from Tony Attwood's website, www.tonyattwood.com.au).

Solutions!

- **The student can be taught a story or the schedule of what is expected at recess.** For example: "Recess: Most days we go to recess three times. Once in the morning, once after lunch, and once in the afternoon. Sometimes recess in on the playground. A lot of the children play on the playground equipment. Everyone should play safely, which means following the playground rules. When the bell rings, that means it is time to line up and go inside. I will try to line up as soon as the bell rings. This will make my teachers happy. After I line up, I will try to stay in line. Everyone will be proud of me!"

- **Offer guidelines or options that are available** to the student if she wants to be alone or in a smaller group environment. Can the student help clean lunch tables or volunteer in another teacher's class?

- Have a peer buddy or aide to assist the student at recess.

- **Establish a safe place or person to turn to** if she needs help.

Behavior?

Problems at Lunchtime

Some students may be over- or under-reactive to noise; some may be over- or under-reactive to things in their mouth. Some of these students may prefer to eat only foods with a certain texture.

The school cafeteria can be overwhelming for people who *don't* have sensory issues. Imagine what it is like for a child who is sensitive to smells, sounds, and sights. Students sensitive to smell may gag or throw up.

$\longrightarrow$

The student may be a messy eater because of fine motor or sensory issues. He may prefer using his fingers rather than utensils because he dislikes the feel or taste of the utensils in his mouth. Or he may be unable to "feel" the utensils in his mouth. Many students on the spectrum have fine motor issues as well, which makes it difficult for the child to use utensils effectively.

As with recess, lunchtime is supposed to be a relaxing time for students. Typical students have conversations while eating. But having a conversation and trying to eat a meal in the cafeteria can both be challenges for some students. They may prefer eating in a quiet, isolated place.

Solutions!

- **Parents need to know the menus for school lunches** so they know when to pack their child's lunch.

- **Work with staff and the student's IEP team to explore alternatives** to the cafeteria. Sitting at the end of a table in the cafeteria or in the office are two examples.

Behavior?

Not Asking for Help

It may be difficult to understand why a student who may need assistance has a hard time asking for help. Some of our disabled students have an aversion to drawing any attention to themselves. Unfortunately, this can sometimes hinder their academic progress. These students may genuinely require assistance, but because of deficits in problem-solving, they "get stuck." They may choose to remain quiet and unnoticed, or lack the communication skills to initiate a request for help.

Solutions!

- Good teachers naturally seek to **initiate communication with students** they know are having difficulty. This is important with the disabled population. By checking with the student frequently during times when you suspect such difficulty, it alleviates the need for the student to initiate the action.

- **Create a signal with the student.** For instance, arrange with them a system in which, if the student places her paper in a particular corner of her desk, it indicates the need for help. Some students may find this nonverbal signal easier to initiate.

- The student must be taught how and when to ask for help. The IEP team may want to **consider setting up guidelines or a story to teach the child how to ask for help.**

Transitioning and the Insistence on Sameness

Among the most common characteristics of a child with Autism Spectrum Disorder or a child with obsessive-compulsive behavior is the insistence on keeping things the same. Once in motion, they will tend to want to continue in the same direction to the exclusion of other directions. This could be the student who refuses to go on to the next activity until he has finished the first activity. It makes going from one task to another very difficult.

This behavior can also be seen in the student who has a hard time if seats are changed or the furniture is rearranged. These students like schedules and hate surprises. They would prefer doing things the same way every day, and can become upset or frustrated if changes are made.

Solutions!

- **A visual schedule is often helpful** in these situations. Knowing that the day will progress from A to B to C is sometimes enough for the student to transition successfully.

- **Prompt the student prior to the transition or a change in routine.** If the student understands what is going to happen a few minutes in advance, then he can mentally prepare for it.

- **Modify the amount of work expected of the student.** If there is a chance that he may not be able to finish a task within a given time, he may have difficulty "letting it go" and moving on. If he can be allowed to do a bit less, this problem may be avoided.

● **Remind the student early in the day** of any expected changes to the usual routine.

● **If possible, allow the student to finish his present task** prior to moving on to the next one. It may be that several students are in a similar situation.

Section Four

Social-Emotional Issues

*R*esearch and observation clearly demonstrate that students with the disabilities we have been discussing tend to be less accepted by peers, interact awkwardly and inappropriately in social situations, and lack social perception. Stephen M. Edelson, Ph.D, classified the social problems into three categories: socially avoidant, socially indifferent, and socially awkward (from the Center for the Study of Autism, www.autism.org).

Socially Avoidant

These individuals avoid virtually all forms of social interaction. When someone tries to interact with them, the most common response is to not respond at all, or walking/running away. For many years, it was thought that this type of reaction to their social environment indicated that these individuals did not like or were fearful of people. Another theory, based on interviews with adults with autism, suggests that the problem may be due to a hypersensitivity to certain sensory stimuli. For example, some state that a parent's voice hurt their ears; some describe the smell of their parents' perfume or cologne as offensive, and others describe pain when being touched or held.

Socially Indifferent

Individuals who are described as "socially indifferent" do not seek social interaction with others (unless they want something), nor do they actively avoid social situations. They do not seem to mind being with people, but at the same time, they do not mind being by themselves. One theory is that these individuals do not obtain "biochemical pleasure" from being with people.

Socially Awkward

These individuals may try very hard to have friends, but they cannot keep them. This problem is common among many students with disabilities. There are two schools of thought. One is that these students have been rejected so often that they have not been able to practice the skills needed to be successful. The other school of thought is that there is a neurological difference that impedes the area of social learning, i.e., they lack reciprocity in their interactions and have poor conversational skills. Many of these students do not learn social skills and social taboos by observing others, and they often lack common sense when making social decisions. This category is the most common.

Behavior?

Saying Rude or Inappropriate Things

*B*ecause of their inability to perceive others' intentions and perspectives, and their impaired capacity to read the gestures and unspoken nuances in everyday social communication, individuals with disabilities may not respond, or may not respond appropriately. This is especially true of those students with Non-verbal Learning Disorder or Autism Spectrum disorders. This is not the result of not caring, but rather it is not responding to what they do not "see."

It would not be uncommon for these students to make comments such as, "It stinks in here," or ask another student, "Why are you weird?" The student may correct the teacher or other classmates with no concern for the other person's feelings. The issue of social inappropriateness is a more difficult problem to overcome. Much of what is needed to assist in this area requires pre-planning by the IEP team.

Solutions!

- **Encourage typical students not to take such statements personally.** This often requires that classmates have an understanding of the child's disability. Parental and IEP team cooperation is needed for this. If students expect that they will occasionally hear such statements from a child with autism, they will be less likely to overreact to them.

- **Shortly after the incident, explain to the student with autism why their statement was**

inappropriate, and offer options for handling such situations in the future. This requires that the student is receiving some kind of counseling so that he or she can expect to be coached by their teacher from time to time, as needed.

● **Consider asking a peer buddy to help teach the student appropriate conversation skills.** The peer buddy is usually someone who is seen as a leader and can be used as a model for the disabled student. Again, cooperation of the family and the IEP team is required to implement this.

It should be noted that while students with a Non-verbal Learning Disorder can offer unintentionally inappropriate comments to peers, they may also overreact to statements made about them or to them. A child may genuinely have a question for the disabled student, such as, "Did you get your hair cut?" However, this may be interpreted by the child with autism as the other student making fun of him. He or she may react by feeling embarrassed or hurt, which can lead to further feelings of isolation.

Clothing Issues

Some students may have sensory issues related to clothing. These issues can manifest themselves in the bathroom, PE, or in the classroom. They may also impact how others see them. A child who is sensitive to touch may wear big, baggy clothes. These students may also hate wearing socks and shoes. Students who are under-reactive to touch may have a hard time "feeling" if their clothes are on correctly, which may give them a sloppy appearance. Also, because of fine motor issues, students may have difficulty fastening their belts, tying their shoes, or even fastening their pants or buttoning a shirt—making going to the bathroom

an issue. A student who is obsessing or perseverating may even want to wear the same clothes every day.

- If the issues are interfering with school activities, **communicate to the parents to see what works at home.** Together, you may come up with a solution such as Velcro as a replacement for shoe strings.

- **Ask the student** specifically what makes them comfortable or uncomfortable and communicate this with the parents.

- The student who is having difficulties such as these may be receiving occupational therapy services to help resolve them. **If the student is receiving OT services, check to make certain that such issues are being addressed.**

Behavior?

Difficulty Accepting Criticism

Students may have difficulty with accepting criticism or being corrected. One hypothesis is that being corrected causes anxiety, thus triggering a strong emotional response that they are ill-equipped to manage. Another hypothesis has to do with these students' tendencies to be perfectionists. In trying to gain control over their environment, some of these students like to be right—all of the time. Minor adjustments to how we approach students with autism can often make the difference in the way criticism is received by them.

Solutions!

● For teachers, it is important to **keep a calm, consistent, and steady voice.** Praise, while certainly appropriate, should not be overdone. The student will understand the words, but may not understand the reason for effusive overtures.

● **Try to "qualify" statements when offering criticism or correction.** Telling a student that he or she has come up an incorrect answer is commonplace in the classroom, but the child with autism may overreact to being told that their answer is "wrong." Consider the following example:

Teacher: Mike, what is 7 x 8?

Mike: 63

Teacher: Close. You would have been correct if I had asked "What is 7 x 9?" Would you like to try another one?

- **If the child is particularly sensitive, writing down your criticism rather than talking may be an avenue to explore.** The student may be better able to process the content of what you are saying because there is less emotion involved. Also, by writing, you are more likely to keep your criticism short and to the point.

- **Encourage classmates to anticipate an occasional unexpected reaction** they might make to the student with the disability. Encourage them to also be steady and consistent with their mannerisms. Again, this may require the cooperation of the family and the IEP team.

Difficulty Making Decisions

Although many students with disabilities in the general education classrooms have average to above-average intelligence, they can lack high-level thinking and comprehension skills. These students tend to be very literal. Their thinking is concrete, and abstract reasoning and problem-solving skills are poor.

Solutions!

- **If the lesson is abstract, offer additional information and simplify it.** These students often do not understand emotional nuances, multiple levels of meaning, and relationship issues.

- **Give students *choices* rather than open-ended questions.** Open-ended questions make heavy demands on word retrieval, organization, and memory. (Hint: these students may do better if the number of choices offered is pared down.)

Excessive Talking

*E*xcessive talking can manifest itself in two ways. The first involves the student who has to tell you everything he knows on a certain subject. These students are fixated or obsessed with a certain thought or subject. Because they do not always understand social rules, and may have limited perception of the feelings or interests of others, they assume that everyone enjoys their subject matter as much as they do. These students have difficulty reading the body language of others, so they do not pick up on cues that indicate others' boredom or frustration. They seem to talk "at" you rather than "to" you, giving information rather

than holding a give-and-take conversation. Sometimes, in an attempt to discuss their desired subject, they talk excessively and will often interrupt. Some of these students may answer rhetorical questions out loud. Some students actually believe the teacher is speaking exclusively to them instead of to the entire class—despite being surrounded by twenty other students.

The second scenario is often interpreted as "attention seeking" on the part of the student. However, this student may be simply "filling time" that the teacher has assigned as "time to start your homework." (Children on the spectrum often have difficulty with unstructured time.) Or this may be the student's way of participating in class, if she cannot otherwise keep up with the rate of discussion. She knows she is expected to participate, but the only way she can do this is on her own terms, and her own topic. She may not be able to keep up with a topic that is under someone else's control.

Both these situations result from a lack of understanding rules that seem apparent to the rest of us. Unfortunately, these students may seem to others as trying to act like a "know-it-all."

Solutions!

● **Be concrete and set specific guidelines.** Telling the student she has a problem with boundaries is not sufficient. Boundaries are defined by appropriateness of physical distance, physical contact, topics of conversation that are off limits, etc. Define what is okay and not okay for her to do. Remind her periodically about these rules—especially when she is spotted breaking them.

● **Do not allow the student to monopolize class discussions.** Let her know that all students are to be given a chance to speak or ask questions, and that she will have other opportunities after everyone has been heard. A gentle reminder of this is often enough.

● **Arrange for another student to periodically initiate conversation with the student** if she is having a difficult time appropriately engaging with other students. This will offer opportunities for practice.

● **Set up a time when the student can talk about her preferred topic.** Allowing the child to have five minutes of conversation time with the teacher or another adult can be used as a reward.

Humming, Talking to Self, or Inappropriate Vocalizations/Odd Gestures

At recess, Jacob does not try to play with other children. Instead, he seems to prefer walking around, talking and laughing to himself. This behavior makes him look very odd, and some of the kids are starting to make fun of him and call him "crazy." Jacob hears the name-calling, but continues his odd behavior. Why?

The student who hums or makes inappropriate vocalizations is often attempting to drown out other, potentially stress-inducing noises or events.

- If the student is humming in a classroom where others are doing a project or assignment that includes talking or other noisy activities, it may be possible to **allow the student to continue.** This is possible if the student is being productive and remaining on task.

- **Use verbal prompts** to remind the student to choose a better time to make such noises.

- **Provide the student with a stress-relief item** such as a squeeze ball as an alternative.

- If deemed appropriate by the IEP team, **teach the other students in class to occasionally expect such behavior by the student.** As they learn about the student's uniqueness, they will be less likely to be surprised by it.

Behavior?

Interrupting

Some students are so rule-governed that, when they feel that someone or something is "breaking the rules," they are obsessed with having it corrected. For example, a teacher who has written the wrong date on the board or made a mistake in addition may not realize why the student is jumping up and down in his seat with his hand raised. He is trying to get the teachers' attention immediately, and won't take "wait" for an answer. He is so obsessed with correcting the error that he cannot concentrate until the mistake has been corrected. This is another behavior that can make the student appear to be a "know-it-all."

Solutions!

- **Do not take correction personally.** To these students, correcting the teacher is simply putting their universe back in order.

- **Be concrete and set specific guidelines.** Telling the student he has a problem with boundaries is not enough. Boundaries are defined by appropriateness of physical distance, physical contact, and topics of conversation that are off-limits, etc. Define what is okay and not okay for him to do. Periodically remind him about these rules—especially when he is spotted breaking them.

- **Arrange with the student** that he will have time after class to discuss any errors he observed. This will give him the outlet while not disrupting the class.

Laughing Excessively or Being Silly

Some students with disabilities are not able to regulate their bodies and emotions—they have difficulty controlling the amount of emotion that comes out. For example, a teacher may be scolding another student, and the student with disabilities starts laughing uncontrollably. Excessive laughter can be such a strong stress-releaser that it overrides the student's understanding that his behavior may be inappropriate.

Solutions!

- **The most effective means of dealing with this behavior is the verbal or visual prompt.** At the onset of this behavior, stand close to the student and remind him of what would be a more appropriate means of expression.

- **Give alternatives to the behavior.** If the student is old enough and has the skills, ask him to write about what he finds amusing and turn it in to you in journal form.

- If prompts are not effective, **arrange for the student to do some other task in the room,** in order to get his mind focused on a goal-oriented task.

- If possible, **arrange for the student to go to his "safe place"** where he can fully express and explain what he found amusing.

Remember, we are sometimes caught between wanting to stop the behavior and knowing that the child is getting a need met. It is not always easy to decide which of these paths to take.

Behavior?

Little or No Eye Contact

We have included this chapter because educators generally view lack of eye contact as the sign of a "problem." Our society often views lack of eye contact as a sign that the person is not listening or is not trustworthy. However, many students with autism resist making eye contact with others even when prompted to do so. Because of poor attention issues, a student may not even look to where others are pointing or looking. Adults with Nonverbal-learning Disorders and Autism Spectrum Disorders have reported that this lack of eye contact is due to one of two factors. The first is that many of these

people do not "read" body language or facial expressions and, therefore, see no reason to look at someone. The second factor could be that looking at someone's face is too overwhelming; they cannot concentrate on what they are saying while also looking at someone's face. Mick said, "I look at an inanimate object. It helps me to think. I can concentrate more if I look at a blank wall, but then people think I am ignoring them" (from Tony Attwood's website, www.tonyattwood.com.au).

Solutions!

- **Continue to prompt the student, but do not insist on eye contact.** This can often cause more problems than it solves.

- **Periodically remind the student of the appropriateness of eye contact during conversation.** Praise them when they remember to use it, e.g., "I like the way you looked at me. It let me know you were listening."

 These students can be taught when and how to look at people. This may be considered as a goal by the IEP team.

Smelling People or Objects

*O*ccasionally, the student with sensory integration issues will attempt to get a sensory need met through
means of taste or smell. These students may choose to lick
a metal object or smell a fellow student to get a need met,
and may not realize the inappropriateness of doing so.

Solutions!

- **Attempt to anticipate such events.** Parents often notice this behavior at home. Request that they keep you informed of such behavior.

- **Remind the student** that it is sometimes inappropriate to smell people or certain objects (although there are certainly times when it is appropriate, such as smelling flowers, etc.).

- **Offer the student access to a replacement sensory input device that is more socially appropriate.** (Please refer to Appendix B for suggestions.)

Behavior?

Talking Loudly

You may notice that some of your students have issues with talking too fast or too loudly. These students may have limited awareness of how their voice sounds to others. The intensity of the sound can be a difficult problem to address, as it is a very abstract concept—and one that is relative, as well.

Solutions!

- **Use a signal.** You could try the universal "quiet" sound (index finger to the lips while saying "Shh"), or another signal that both of you agree upon. Some people also use the phrases, "indoor voice" to signify the quiet voice, and "outdoor voice" to signify the louder voice.

- **Use a visual cue such as an index card so the student can keep it in front of him as a "reminder."** If she reduces the intensity of her voice, you should reinforce her with, "Good job! I like your quiet voice" or another positive response.

- If it remains an issue, **work with staff and the student's IEP team. The speech-language pathologist may have other suggestions.**

Behavior?

Temper Outbursts

Temper tantrums are among the most difficult issues for teachers to work through. They are made more difficult if the student has autism, because once he has passed a "point of no return," he is less likely to follow directions.

Solutions!

- **Attempt to anticipate the event.** Put a quick stop to teasing or bullying if possible. If you can predict the occurrence, a goal-directed task may act as a diversion from the problem

- If the student has already had the outburst, **give him choices rather than directives.** While students having temper outbursts can be difficult to "reach," giving them a choice is often more productive than forcing them to obey a directive. For example, you can say, "Pete, you can either sit at your desk or get a drink of water."

- **Utilize calming techniques** as described in Appendix C.

Keep in mind that when a student with autism has entered a highly emotional or stressful state, he may not be able to communicate his needs for as long as several hours afterward. Occasionally these students are able to write about their needs before they verbalize them—but avoid trying to force them to answer. Note: Continued temper outbursts should be discussed with site administrator and school psychologist to develop an appropriate behavior plan.

Appendix A: Movement Breaks/ Goal-Directed Tasks

- **Ask the student to run an errand** or offer to allow her to go outside and get a drink or use the restroom.

- **Direct the student to do a manual task in the class-room.** For example: passing out papers, stapling, putting away books, backpacks or play equipment, erasing the whiteboard, stapling, hole-punching papers, or sorting homework/papers into files or boxes.

- **Assign a second desk** to the student where she could sit during different parts of the day to avoid sitting in one place for too long.

- **Have the student do Isometric exercises** such as hand-clasps or wall push-ups (pushing against a wall).

- **Have the student go into the playground for a specific purpose,** such as hanging from bars, doing jumping jacks, swinging, or climbing on playground equipment.

● Have the student bounce or do push-ups on a therapy ball.

● **Allow the student to stand at his desk** to help him stay alert during periods of prolonged sitting.

Appendix B: Sensory Input Devices

● **Squeeze-balls** (small, hand-held balls filled with gel or sand to give needed sensory feedback). Koosh® Balls also serve this purpose.

● **"Fidget" toys,** such as Silly Putty® or Theraputty™. Paper clips can be used for manipulation by older students. Tangles or other small, plastic, twistable toys for students to manipulate into shapes. These pliable objects offer enough resistance to meet the sensory needs of the student.

● **Movin' Sit or Disc'O'Sit chair cushions** (made by Gymnic®), designed to allow the student to move in their chair without leaving it. These are inflatable discs with texture on one side. Enough air is added so the child may wiggle slightly, which aids focus and attention.

- **Weighted objects** (vests, pillows, blankets, lap pads, stuffed animals, wrist- or ankle-wraps). These should be used under the supervision of an OT.

- **Therapy Balls.** These are inflatable balls, usually large enough to sit on or do push-ups with.

- **Chewy foods**, such as granola bars, bagels, cheese, gum, licorice, Fruit Roll-ups®, Starburst® candies, and Tootsie Rolls®. Chewy foods offer resistance that can be organizing and help to meet sensory needs.

- **Crunchy foods,** such as dry cereal, pretzels, granola bars, vegetables, popcorn, and potato chips.

- **Sour foods,** such as lemon balls, sour balls, and Mega Warheads™. Like crunchy foods, sour foods are alerting, arousing, and organizing.

- **Water bottles**.

Appendix C: Calming Techniques

- **Direct the student to a predetermined quiet place.** Temporary solitude can be restorative. Students can use this time to calm their bodies and their minds.

- **Direct the student to use the music center.** This could be a corner of your classroom or simply an IPod that is used for this purpose.

- **Direct the student to do deep breathing** (take several deep breaths and hold to the count of five before exhaling).

Additional Resources

1001 Great Ideas for Teaching and Raising Children with Autism or Asperger's, Revised and Expanded 2nd Edition
By Ellen Notbohm and Veronica Zysk
ISBN: 9781935274063

Answers to Questions Teachers Ask about Sensory Integration: Forms, Checklists, and Practical Tools
By Carol Kranowitz and Stacey Szklut
ISBN: 9781932565461

Basic Skills Checklists: Teacher-friendly Assessment for Students with Autism or Special Needs
By Marlene Breitenbach
ISBN: 9781932565751

The CAT-kit: The new Cognitive Affective Training program for improving communication!
By Tony Attwood, Kirsten Callesen, and Annette Moller Nielson
ISBN: 9781932565737

Building Bridges through Sensory Integration: Therapy for Children with Autism and other Pervasive Developmental Disorders
By Paula Aquilla and Shirley Sutton
ISBN: 9781932565454

How Do I Teach This Kid?: Visual Work Tasks for Beginning Learners on the Autism Spectrum
By Kimberly Henry
ISBN: 9781932565249

Inclusive Programming for Elementary Students with Autism
By Sheila Wagner
ISBN: 9781885477545

Inclusive Programming for High School Students with Autism or Asperger's Syndrome
By Sheila Wagner
ISBN: 9781932565577

Inclusive Programming for Middle School Students with Autism or Asperger's Syndrome
By Sheila Wagner
ISBN: 9781885477842

Learning in Motion: 101+ Sensory Activities for the Classroom
By Patricia Angermeier and Joan Krzyzanowski
ISBN: 9781932565904

My Friend with Autism: A Children's Book for Peers
By Beverly Bishop and Craig Bishop
ISBN: 9781885477897

The New Social Story Book, Revised and Expanded 10th Anniversary Edition: Over 150 Social Stories that Teach Everyday Social Skills to Children with Autism or Asperger's Syndrome, and Their Peers
By Carol Gray
ISBN: 9781935274056

No More Meltdowns: Positive strategies for managing and preventing out-of-control behavior
By Jed Baker
ISBN: 9781932565621

Sensitive Sam: Sam's sensory adventure has a happy ending!
By Marla Roth-Fisch
ISBN: 9781932565867

Squirmy Wormy: How I Learned to Help Myself
By Lynda Farrington Wilson
ISBN: 9781935567189

The Social Skills Picture Book: Teaching Play, Emotion, and Communication to Children with Autism
By Jed Baker
ISBN: 9781885477910

Ten Things Every Child with Autism Wishes You Knew
By Ellen Notbohm
ISBN: 9781932565300

Ten Things Your Student with Autism Wishes You Knew
By Ellen Notbohm
ISBN: 9781932565362

A Treasure Chest of Behavioral Strategies for Individuals with Autism
By Beth Fouse and Maria Wheeler
ISBN: 9781885477361

Ultimate Guide to Sensory Processing Disorder: Easy, Everyday Solutions to Sensory Challenges
by Roya Ostovar
ISBN: 9781935274070

Understanding Asperger's Syndrome, Fast Facts: A Guide for Teachers and Educators to Address the Needs of the Student
By Emily Burrows and Sheila Wagner
ISBN: 9781932565157

All resources are available in bookstores everywhere, Amazon.com, and on the publisher's website www.FHautism.com.

About the Authors

Beth Aune is the owner-therapist of Desert Occupational Therapy for Kids, Inc., a pediatric outpatient clinic in Palm Desert, California. Beth and her team of dedicated and passionate professionals provide assessment and intervention for at-risk children with a variety of diagnoses, including: autism spectrum disorder, sensory processing disorder, developmental delay, feeding dysfunction, Down syndrome, ce-

rebral palsy, and others. Desert OT for Kids, Inc. provides skilled intervention in the clinic, school, and home settings. Beth is a co-author of *Behavior Solutions for the Inclusive Classroom* (2010) and *Behavior Solutions In and Beyond the Inclusive Classroom* (2011), and sole author of *Behavior Solutions for the Home and the Community* (2013). She is a knowledgeable, fervent, and energetic speaker throughout the nation on the topic of identifying, understanding, and treating children's problematic behaviors and sensory issues. Her presentations, workshops, and books offer practical solutions and strategies for teachers and parents to implement in the school, home, and community settings. Beth is a clinical instructor for Loma Linda University School of Allied Health Professions and is on the advisory board for the Masters of OT program. She is a board member for Future Horizons, Inc., a major publisher for the autism and sensory processing disorder community.

Beth Burt resides in Southern California with her husband, their two sons, two cats and a dog. Due to her experiences with her own children, one with an autism spectrum disorder (ASD) and the other with a learning disability, Beth became a passionate advocate in improving education, life, and employment opportunities for individuals with ASD and other disorders. She serves on the board of a number of  non-profit organizations which assist children, teen and adults with special needs, and continues to work on various issues and public policy effecting individuals with disabilities. She speaks frequently in the Southern California area to colleges, parent groups, non-profit organizations, government agencies, and businesses.

Peter Gennaro is currently a special education school teacher for the Alvord Unified School District in southern California. He previously served as Director of Special Education in the same district. He has taught classes for students with mild to moderate disabilities as well as students with emotional disturbance. He works closely with students, teachers, and families and considers education to be the most direct way to help children succeed.

Index